THE NATIONAL TRUST
Little Library

Coffee

JILL NORMAN

DORLING KINDERSLEY
LONDON • NEW YORK • STUTTGART

A DORLING KINDERSLEY BOOK

EDITOR MARK RONAN

SENIOR EDITOR CAROLYN RYDEN

DESIGN MATHEWSON BULL

PHOTOGRAPHER DAVE KING

FIRST PUBLISHED IN GREAT BRITAIN IN 1992
BY DORLING KINDERSLEY LIMITED
9 HENRIETTA STREET, LONDON WC2E 8PS

TEXT COPYRIGHT © 1992 JILL NORMAN
ILLUSTRATION COPYRIGHT © 1992
DORLING KINDERSLEY LIMITED

A CIP CATALOGUE RECORD FOR THIS BOOK IS AVAILABLE
FROM THE BRITISH LIBRARY.

ISBN 0-86318-788-9

PRINTED AND BOUND IN HONG KONG
BY IMAGO

CONTENTS

CULTIVATING COFFEE

T̶HERE are times of great beauty on a coffee-farm. When the plantation flo-wered in the beginning of the rains, it was a radiant sight, like a cloud of chalk, in the mist and drizzling rain, over six hundred acres of land. The coffee-blossom has a delicate slightly bitter scent, like the blackthorn blossom. When the field red-dened with the ripe berries, all the women and children, whom they called Totos, were called out to pick the coffee off the trees, together with the men; then the wagons and carts brought it down to the factory near the river ... The big coffee-dryer turned and turned, rumbling the coffee in its iron belly with a sound like pebbles that are washed about on the sea-shore ... Later on the coffee was hulled, graded and sorted by hand, and packed in sacks sewn up with a saddler's needle ... The coffee would be on the sea in a day or two, and we could only hope for good luck at the big auction-sales in London.'
Karen Blixen, Out of Africa, 1917.

The coffee plant is a small evergreen tree, extensively cultivated in the humid tropics. The Coffea arabica species, which produces the best coffee, is indigenous to Ethiopia, but it crossed the Red Sea to the Yemen in southern Arabia at an early date and has long been cultiv-ated in the mountains there. Of some 60 species of coffee, only two others are cultivated extensively: C. canephora var. robusta, a hardy, heavy-cropping species, and C. liberica, a vigorous variety. Production of C. liberica is very small; robusta, which is used in some cheaper blends and in instant coffee, is more important.

C. arabica *is usually grown as a shrub. It bears fruit at three or four years, and will go on producing for about 25 years. There are two or three crops a year, for the coffee tree bears blossom, unripe and ripe fruits simultaneously. The white flowers, fragrant as jasmine, are fragile and ephemeral; in a day or two they fade. The fruits, called cherries, must be picked at the moment of optimum ripeness; too ripe*

Arbre du Café dessiné en ... Arabie sur le Naturel

Coffee tree

and the beans, the seeds within them, are spoiled; unripe and they are wasted, for the beans will not ripen once picked. The cherries turn from green to yellow, to red and finally a deep red-black, when they are ripe and ready to be picked. A tree yields 4–6 lb/ 2–3 kg of fruit a year, which in turn gives about 1–1^1/$_2$lb/ 500–750 g green beans, and 20 percent less still when they are roasted. Harvest-ing is done by hand, and is an expensive business because the pickers must return several times to the same tree. Each fruit usually contains two beans in a parchment-like envelope; varieties with a single round bean, or berry, are called peaberry coffees. The best coffees are washed and the pulp is lar-gely removed, then they are piled up to ferment; when the remaining flesh rots it is washed off and the beans are dried. In a simpler, cheaper process the cherries are spread in the sun to dry for three weeks or dried artificially, then the shrivelled skins are removed. Now the green beans are ready for grading and shipping.

COFFEE IN THE MIDDLE EAST

*O*UR WORD *'coffee'* derives from the Arabic qahwah, *one of the words originally used for wine, which came to mean coffee. Coffee beans used to be chewed before it was discovered they could be ground and boiled with water to make a drink. No one knows when or where coffee was first drunk, although it seems that plantations existed in the Yemen by the 15th century. The most reliable early records would suggest that coffee was first drunk by the Sufis.*

Constantinople coffee house

Muslim mystics, the Sufis discovered that coffee could ward off sleep and stimulate mental activity, thus aiding their devotions. Through their ordinary daily lives coffee drinking spread to urban centres. By the end of the 15th century traders and pilgrims took coffee to Mecca and eventually to all parts of the Islamic world. Although still used by Sufis in their ceremonies, the less pious found coffee an agreeable stimulus to conversation, and the coffee house was born.

These became popular gathering places, offering entertainment, music and dancing, and a congenial atmosphere. But coffee also excited the drinker, and was said to provoke political argument and subversive plots. Soon both imams and temporal rulers were opposed to coffee

Turkish coffee grinder

and sought to close the coffee houses, on the grounds that they were places of corruption. Attempts were made to claim that coffee was one of the beverages forbidden by Islamic law, although it is not mentioned in the Quran. Edicts and decrees were to be successful for a brief period, then coffee drinking and coffee houses returned until the next ban. Although women did not go out in public, they took to coffee as well, drinking it at home with their companions.

Middle Eastern coffee pot

Arab coffee-drinkers playing backgammon

COFFEE
IN EUROPE

*C*OFFEE REACHED EUROPE *from Constantinople in the 17th century. In 1615 the Italian traveller, Pietro della Valle, described a hot black drink, refreshing in summer and warming in winter, which the Turks sipped slowly with their companions. He noted that it was called* cahve *and was made with the fruit or seed of a tree growing in Arabia.*

Coffee begins its long journey to Europe

A year later, a Dutch boat put in at the Yemeni port of Mocha en route to the Indies. One of the passengers, a Mr van den Broek, who travelled in the hinterland, discovered coffee too: 'It is a kind of black beans ... of which they make a black water and drink warm'.

The Venetians were responsible for bringing coffee to Europe.

At first it was sold by pharmacists, but made little impact until the first coffee shop opened and instructions circulated about how to roast and grind coffee and the addition of spices or sugar – but not milk.

Once coffee was established, its spread across the continent was swift, but as in the Middle East it also aroused hostility. In 1674 *The Women's Petition Against Coffee* was published in London, complaining that 'it made men as unfruitful as deserts whence that unhappy berry is said to be brought'. The men wrote a reply 'vindicating their own Performances, and the Vertues of their liquor, from the Undeserved Aspersions lately cast upon them'. In France Louis XIV gave the exclusive right to sell coffee to one supplier in exchange for a substantial contribution to the treasury; unfortunately this raised the price so much that consumption declined and the merchant faced bankruptcy. Frederick the Great made money out of coffee by only permitting it to be roasted in royal establishments, thus obliging the well-to-do to buy at high prices from the state.

Coffee trading at a Middle Eastern port

European noblemen in an 18th-century café

THE COFFEE HOUSE

*C*OFFEE MADE *its appearance in Paris in 1657 and was sold in little shops by coffee brewers, by street vendors and at fair booths. The first true café was opened by François Procope in 1686. Its elegant tapestries, mirrors and marble tables made it respectable and fashionable; people flocked to hear the gossip, see the actors from the Comédie Française or read the papers.*

The Procope soon had hundreds of imitators. In Vienna and Budapest coffee houses developed from habits acquired during the Turkish occupation, when a crowd gathered where the itinerant coffee vendor made his fire. The barber shaved heads, and the travelling storyteller brought the news and gossip, essential when few people could read. The first coffee house opened in London in 1652, and by 1675 Charles II tried to close 'these resorts of disaffected persons' who disturbed 'the peace and quiet of the nation'.

Early London coffee house

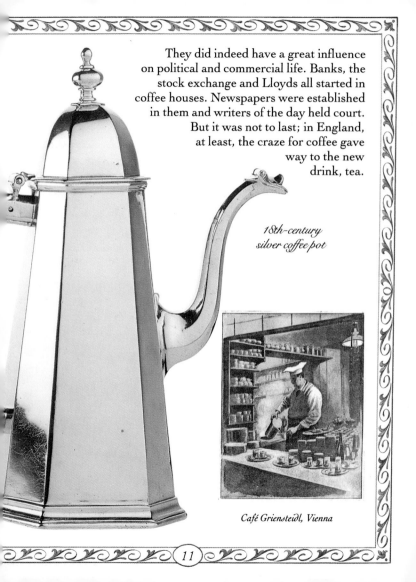

They did indeed have a great influence on political and commercial life. Banks, the stock exchange and Lloyds all started in coffee houses. Newspapers were established in them and writers of the day held court. But it was not to last; in England, at least, the craze for coffee gave way to the new drink, tea.

18th-century silver coffee pot

Café Griensteidl, Vienna

COFFEE-PRODUCING
COUNTRIES

*T*HE ARABS GUARDED *their exclusive trade in coffee jealously for almost 100 years. Then in 1690, the Dutch, already in control of the spice trade from the East, succeeded in getting seedlings to plant in Java. The coffee tree adapts easily to new environments, and plantations were soon established through the Dutch eastern colonies. By the 1750s they were sending more than 3,000lb/ 1,400 kg of coffee a year to Amsterdam.*

French advertisement c.1890

Coffee-producing regions of the world

A young French officer introduced the first plant into Martinique about 1715; this tree was to be the source of all the coffee plantations of the New World.

Coffee spread rapidly to Guyana and Surinam, throughout the Caribbean islands and Central America. By the middle of the century Portuguese settlers had huge plantations in the valleys behind Rio; the soils were

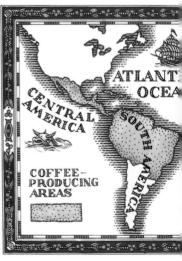

12

fertile, little capital was needed and there was plenty of slave labour. A coffee empire was created. But 100 years on, the soil was exhausted, diseases had struck the trees and slavery was abolished. The planters of Rio struggled to keep their position, but the centre of coffee production moved to São Paulo, situated inland at an altitude where the coffee tree flourished better.

By the end of the 19th century demand for coffee was great and plantations spread rapidly in the European colonies of tropical Africa. The Ivory Coast, Angola and Uganda became important producers on a world scale; by the 1940s *robusta* coffee had replaced *arabica* in much of Africa because it is a species less prone to disease.

Today Brazil, Colombia and the Ivory Coast head the 50-odd producer countries that provide the 60 million kg of coffee we drink each year.

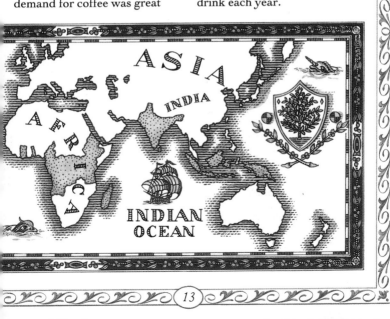

BEAN VARIETIES

Coffee plant

*M*ANY OF THE COFFEES *on sale are blends of beans from different countries, but specialist shops stock pure coffees. It can be fun to try different coffees and it is easy to experiment and make your own blends. Choose coffee to suit the time of day: a light coffee for breakfast and a strong, dark roast for after dinner.*

Colombian coffees vary in quality; the best have a full, rich flavour. Medellin has good acidity, a clean aroma and is strong without being bitter, while Excelso is somewhat nutty. The best plantations are in the foothills of the Andes.

Colombian Medellin

Maragogipe

Earlier this century a tree near the village of Maragogipe in Brazil was found to have mutated to produce very large beans. Cuttings were introduced in Mexico and Guatemala. The beans have a fine acidity and are best medium roasted.

Kenyan coffees have piquancy, fine acidity and aroma and a fruity, mild flavour. They blend well with other coffees. Small round peaberry coffees are good for home roasting because the beans have a regular shape.

Blue Mountain is the best Jamaican coffee. High grown, it has fine acidity and a rich nuttiness. It is prized by connoisseurs for its mellow, delicate, yet full aroma and flavour. It benefits from a medium roast.

Cuban coffee is sweet, mellow and aromatic, and full-bodied with a subtle smoky note of cedarwood in the taste. A medium roast brings out the rich flavours. Little seen in Europe or North America, Cuban coffee is sought after by the Japanese.

Kenyan Peaberry   *Blue Mountain*   *Cuban*

UNUSUAL COFFEES

HAWAIIAN KONA KAI: the volcanic soils of the Kona region produce a fine, subtly flavoured, fruity coffee with light acidity and a heady aroma.

MONSOON MYSORE: from southern India. Monsoon winds pass over the unwashed coffee stacks, turning the beans golden. The flavour is mild and velvety.

Hawaiian Kona Kai

Sumatra Mandheling

YEMENI MOCHA: organically grown beans with an irregular shape. This coffee has a wine-like, gamey flavour and good acidity.

SUMATRA MANDHELING: a full-bodied coffee with low acidity and a rich aroma and taste, brought out by a darker roast.

ST. HELENA: this tiny Atlantic island produces a delicate but rich coffee appreciated for its rounded taste and light underlying acidity.

OLD JAVA: the green beans are matured for up to three years, giving smoothness and body. Flavour and aroma are rich and earthy with a hint of sweetness.

Monsoon Mysore

St. Helena

Yemeni Mocha

Old Java

ROASTING COFFEE

FRESH COFFEE BEANS are blue-green, grey-green, or occasionally yellow-brown, and have little flavour or aroma. The roasting process transforms them, not only in colour, but also brings out their subtle odours and flavours. Roasts may be dark, medium or light; the best coffees are usually the most lightly roasted, to preserve their mild flavours.

During roasting, the coffee beans are turned constantly, generally in a revolving drum. Commercial roasting machines operate at high temperatures and can roast beans very swiftly, but an experienced professional roaster is still needed to supervise the process.

As the colour of the beans darkens, steam is given off and the coffee smell begins to emerge. The roasted beans lose about 20 percent of their original weight and have a shiny surface because of the oils released during roasting. The darker the roast, the more carbonized and brittle the bean. Once roasted, the beans must be cooled as fast as possible to reduce the loss of essential oils, which are drawn off more quickly while the beans are hot.

Coffee roasting in 19th-century New York

Over-roasted coffee has a bitter flavour and loses its aroma. Fine *arabicas* grown at high altitudes have a delicate acidity which is enhanced by light roasting. A higher roast reduces not only the acidity but also the aroma. Spices may be added to the coffee towards the end of the roasting time, as is done in Ethiopia; ginger, cinnamon and cloves are perhaps the best. Pale roasts are good for coffee to be drunk with milk and darker roasts are better drunk black; very dark glossy beans are the classic style for making strong, bitter espresso. Freshly roasted coffee tastes much better than coffee that has been stored, for the essential oils continue to be lost in storage and aroma and flavour diminish. Coffee can be roasted in the oven or in a heavy pan, but it is a slow, imperfect process, requiring constant supervision. A number of small domestic roasters are now available, and if you really appreciate good coffee you will find it worthwhile roasting your own beans.

Fresh unroasted beans

Pale roast

Medium roast

Dark roast

Full roast

GRINDING COFFEE

*C*OFFEE IS BEST GROUND *just before it is used because grinding breaks open the cells of the bean, releasing the aromatic oils and gases. Once this happens aroma and flavour start to deteriorate. If you buy ground coffee, choose a vacuum pack, or buy in small amounts and keep in a cool place.*

Finely ground coffee keeps its aroma longer than coarsely ground, because the particles form a dense mass with less room for air to enter and cause oxidation and loss of aroma. A fine grind has a high and swift yield because it is in more

Coarse grounds

Medium grounds

contact with the water, whereas the yield from a coarse grind is lower, so more coffee and a longer brewing time are needed for a similar yield.

It is important to have coffee ground to the right degree of fineness for the method used to make it. A coarse grind is needed for the drip method, for making coffee in a jug and for percolators that pump water through the coffee.

A medium grind works well with the plunger method; a medium fine grind is best for the vacuum method and for Moka Express-type steam pressure pots.

Finely ground coffee is needed for paper filters and for espresso coffee.

Pulverized, or powdered, coffee is used for Turkish coffee; sometimes the beans are still pounded with a pestle and mortar in the Middle East. Pulverized coffee has a more intense flavour than coarser grinds, but it can be murky.

Fine grounds

Pulverized coffee

METHODS OF PREPARING COFFEE

'*THE ESSENTIAL QUALITIES of coffee are extracted in the short time following its initial infusion with boiling water; a prolonged infusion does not result in a better liquor.*' Law's Grocer's Manual, *1950*.

It goes on: 'The temperature of the water is very important; actual boiling increases the bitterness of the liquor and long infusion even at lower temperatures has a similar effect, whilst in both cases the flavour and aroma are impaired.'

Viennese coffee

Espresso

These principles apply whatever method is used to make coffee. Delicate coffees are best made by infusion, either by steeping and then straining the coffee, or by the drip method. Strength can be varied by changing the amount of coffee used.

The intense heat of an espresso machine releases the astringent properties of the coffee more swiftly, and the steam released can be used to heat milk to make a frothy cappuccino.

Thick, bitter Turkish coffee, always drunk black, but often sweetened, is made by boiling the coffee and water together and serving unstrained.

Café au lait

Turkish coffee

FLAVOURED COFFEES

*I*N THE MIDDLE EAST *it has long been the custom to flavour coffee with spices. Exotica like ambergris may no longer be used, but cardamom or nutmeg, cinnamon or cloves are often added to the pot. In Ethiopia and Eritrea ginger is the preferred spice. The Mexicans make a heady, rich coffee with cinnamon and cloves. To make your own spiced coffee, grind together a mixture of some or all of these spices and add it to medium roasted coffee as you grind it. Use 1 oz/25 g to 1 lb/500 g coffee.*

Vanilla pod

Cardamom pods

Cinnamon sticks

Ground nutmeg

Brandy

Nutmeg

Additives like chicory root, once used to eke out coffee when it was in short supply or too costly, are rare today, but coffees now come ready-flavoured with essences of vanilla or chocolate, hazelnut or brandy.

PROCESSED COFFEES

*S*OLUBLE COFFEE *was invented at the turn of the century, but did not come into its own until the First World War when it was appreciated for its convenience by the armed forces. Extraction techniques have improved since then, and freeze-drying produces the best quality instant coffees. The aroma cannot match that of freshly made coffee, but the taste of some is getting closer to the real thing. Instant coffee is blended from high-yielding* robusta *coffees, primarily those grown in Africa.*

Advertisement for decaffeinated coffee c.1950

Freeze-dried coffee

Coffee granules

Instant coffee powder

All coffees contain caffeine, *robustas* more than *arabicas*. It can be removed from the unroasted beans by flushing with a chemical solvent or with water. In poor-quality decaffeinated coffees the flavouring constituents are often removed too.

Recipes

*All the recipes are for 4,
but some will serve more*

MEXICAN COFFEE

In Mexico this spiced coffee is
made in an earthenware pot, but
a saucepan can be used instead.

For each person take *¼ pint/
150 ml water, 2 tablespoons coarsely
ground dark coffee, brown sugar* to
taste and *a small piece of cinnamon
stick*. Bring to the boil and
remove from the heat. Stir and
return to the heat. When it
comes to the boil again, strain
and serve.

TURKISH COFFEE

'The coffee powder must be fine enough to pass through the finest sieve. Water and coffee, in the ratio of ten to one are placed in a silver canister, then returned to a very slow fire for the duration of three paternosters. He who likes delicate tastes should add a little sugar, cedar-bark or violet root to the coffee, which sweetens it and makes it aromatic. Coffee made in this way will clear the mind and keep the stomach in order.'

From the memoirs of Count Marsigli, an Italian who was a Turkish prisoner from 1683–5.

Turkish coffee is usually made in a small, long-handled pot made of tinned copper or aluminium, but a small saucepan can be used instead. For each person take *2 fl oz/50 ml water, 1 teaspoon pulverized coffee* and *1/2 teaspoon sugar*. Put the water in the pot and stir in the coffee and sugar. Place over medium heat. When the coffee froths and rises to the rim, remove the pot from the heat and rap the pot sharply to settle the grounds. Return the pot to the heat and repeat twice more, then pour into the cup, making sure some of the froth is on the top.

Variations

In some Arab countries spices are added to the coffee: *bruised cardamom pods, a cinnamon stick* or *a few cloves*. Elsewhere *orange flower water* may be offered so you can add a drop or two to your coffee.

VIENNESE COFFEE
¹/₄ pint/150 ml whipping cream
1 tablespoon icing sugar
1 pint/600 ml strong coffee
1 tablespoon cocoa powder

Whip the cream until it stands in soft peaks, adding the sugar gradually. Chill until ready to serve. Pour the coffee into cups, put a swirl of the whipped cream on top and sprinkle with cocoa.

CAFÉ LIÈGEOIS
Make *¹/₄ pint/150 ml* very strong black coffee, sweeten with *1 tablespoon sugar*, cool and then chill. Whip *¹/₄ pint/150 ml chilled whipping cream* and *2 tablespoons caster sugar* until it stands in peaks. Put *2 scoops Mocha Ice Cream* (see p. 31) into each of 4 tall dessert glasses. Pour over a little of the coffee, then top with whipped cream and a few *chocolate-covered coffee beans*.

CAFÉ BRULOT

'Soak the *peel of a fresh orange* in *rum* (or *brandy*) with *cinnamon, cloves, allspice* and *sugar* to taste. After the peel, spices and sugar have been well steeped in the spirit warm this and set it alight. Then add hot *black coffee*, let it simmer a little and serve.'
The Tenth Muse, Sir Harry Luke, 1962

SPICED ICED COFFEE

2 cinnamon sticks
6 cloves
6 allspice berries
3 tablespoons sugar
1 1/2 pints/900 ml very strong coffee
crushed ice

Add the spices and sugar to the coffee, cover and leave to infuse. When cool, put in the refrigerator and chill for at least 1 hour. Before serving, remove the spices and whisk the coffee at high speed with the ice for a minute or two to produce a smooth, frothy drink. Serve at once.

CREMAT
This coffee is a Catalan speciality.

1/2 pint/300 ml Spanish brandy
1/4 pint/150 ml light rum
2 cinnamon sticks
peel of 1 lemon
6 sugar lumps
1 pint/600 ml strong coffee

Put the brandy, rum, cinnamon, lemon peel and sugar in a pan and heat slowly. Ignite – and stand back because it will flare up. Let it burn for 10 minutes or so, until the liquid has reduced by at least a third, and the flames are much lower. Put a lid over the pan to extinguish them, then pour in the hot coffee, strain and serve.

COFFEE WITH RUM

6 cloves
1 stick cinnamon
4 sugar lumps
peel of 1 orange
3 fl oz/75 ml rum
1/2 pint/300 ml strong coffee

Put the spices, sugar and orange peel in a small pan and pour over the rum – there should be enough just to cover them. Heat gently, shaking the pan, until the sugar has melted. Pour in the hot coffee, strain and serve.

IRISH COFFEE

For each person put *2 tablespoons Irish whiskey* into a glass. Fill almost to the top with *hot coffee* and add *sugar* to taste. Over the back of a spoon pour a layer of cold *double cream* which should stay on top of the coffee. Drink through the cream.

EL CARAJILLO

Many rural communities where work starts very early have their own version of this spiked coffee to get things going. In Normandy they use Calvados, in Yugoslavia, slivovitz, in Spain it is either dry anisette or brandy.

Add *1 tablespoon alcohol*, and *sugar* if you wish, to a cup of *black coffee*.

COFFEE RATAFIA

Grind *4 oz/125 g very dark roast coffee* and use to make *1/2 pint/ 300 ml coffee*. Sweeten it with *8 oz/250g sugar*, and leave to cool. Add *1 pint/600 ml rum* to the coffee. Strain through muslin, bottle and leave for 2 months before drinking.

GRANITA DI CAFFÈ

This is a refreshing summer ice. Make a syrup with *4 oz/125 g sugar* and *³/₄ pint/450 ml water*. Add *¹/₂ pint/300 ml very strong coffee* and leave to cool. Freeze in ice trays until ice crystals form around the edges, then stir, breaking the crystals. Return to the freezer and repeat the stirring every 30 minutes or so, until the granita is all frozen crystals. It will take 2–3 hours. Serve the granita in tall glasses, topped with *whipped cream*.

MOCHA ICE CREAM

³/₄ pint/450 ml single cream
6 oz/175 g vanilla sugar
2 oz/50 g coffee beans, coarsely ground
4 egg yolks
¹/₄ pint/150 ml double cream

Bring the single cream almost to the boil, remove from the heat and stir in half the sugar and the coffee. Cover and infuse for 10 minutes, then strain through a fine sieve or piece of muslin. Beat the egg yolks with the remaining sugar until they are pale. Heat the cream again, whisk a little into the eggs, then add the egg mixture to the cream. Put the pan back on low heat and stir until the custard coats the back of the spoon. Make sure it doesn't boil. Whip the double cream lightly, fold into the custard and freeze in an ice cream machine, following the manufacturer's instructions.

Variations

Add *³/₄ teaspoon ground cinnamon* or *¹/₂ teaspoon ground cardamom* with the ground coffee.

COFFEE PARFAIT

7 fl oz/200 ml milk
3 tablespoons instant coffee
6 oz/175 g sugar
6 egg yolks
1/2 pint/300 ml double cream

Scald the milk, remove from the heat and add the coffee and half the sugar. Cover and leave to stand for 10 minutes. Whisk the egg yolks and remaining sugar together until the yolks are pale. Return the milk to the heat; when it is hot, pour a little onto the eggs, beating as you do so. Now pour this mixture into the milk pan, and cook gently over low heat, stirring all the time. Do not let it boil. Remove from the heat when the custard coats the back of the spoon, and continue to beat as it cools. Whip the double cream until it forms soft peaks then fold it into the coffee mixture. Turn into a mould or soufflé dish, cover and freeze for 3–4 hours, until firm.

BLACK COFFEE JELLY

'30 lumps of sugar
5 tablespoons of water
1 pint of strong black coffee
4 leaves of gelatine [¹/₂ oz/15 g]

Make a syrup with the sugar and water boiled together. Add the coffee to the syrup and stiffen it with the gelatine. Pour it into a mould and allow it to get cold. Serve with whipped cream.'

More Lovely Food, Ruth Lowinsky, 1935

COFFEE AND OATMEAL ICE CREAM

This ice has a texture similar to that of brown bread ice cream.

³/₄ pint/450 ml double cream
4 oz/125 g caster sugar
4 fl oz/125 ml strong coffee
4 oz/125 g coarse oatmeal

Whisk the cream with the sugar and coffee until it thickens, then freeze the mixture in a tray until the sides and bottom are firm. Toast the oatmeal in a medium oven, 190°C/375°F/gas 5, for about 10 minutes, until it is quite dry but not browned. Turn the ice cream out into a chilled bowl, beat for a minute or two, then stir in the oatmeal and return to the freezer until ready to serve.

COFFEE AND PISTACHIO CREAM

Chop *8 oz/250 g pistachio kernels* and soak them in *2 tablespoons brandy* for 10 minutes. Make *¹/₄ pint/150 ml very strong coffee* and heat it gently with *³/₄ pint/450 ml double cream* and *2 beaten egg yolks*.

Add the nuts and stir continuously as the cream heats. Do not let it come to the boil. When the cream has thickened pour it into a bowl and leave to get cold. Sprinkle with more pistachios before serving.

Mocha Diplomate

This recipe comes from *Coffee*,
Claudia Roden, 1977.

4 oz/125 g hazelnuts
5 tablespoons caster sugar
1/2 pint/300 ml double cream
1/4 pint/150 ml single cream
1 heaped tablespoon instant coffee
3 packets boudoir biscuits
coffee with milk

Brown the hazelnuts in a dry frying pan over medium heat until their skins begin to loosen. Remove from the heat and when they are cool enough, rub the nuts between your hands to get rid of the skins. Add 3 tablespoons sugar and return the pan to the heat. When the sugar is melted and lightly browned, stir in the hazelnuts and coat them with the sugar. Pour onto a lightly oiled tray. When the mixture is cool, break into pieces. Keep a few whole hazelnuts for a garnish and make a praline by reducing the rest to a powder in a processor or with a pestle and mortar.

Beat the two creams together, add 2 tablespoons sugar and the coffee dissolved in a tablespoon of warm water. Moisten the biscuits by dipping them briefly in the milky coffee. Put a layer of biscuits in an 8 in/20 cm tin, preferably one with detachable sides. Spread with a thin layer of cream and sprinkle with a little praline. Repeat the layers until all the biscuits are used up, ending with a layer of cream. Spread a layer of cream around the sides, sprinkle praline all over and place the hazelnuts on top.
Freeze for 3–4 hours to give a semi-frozen texture.

FROZEN COFFEE DESSERT

4 oz/125 g brown sugar
4 fl oz/125 ml coffee
1 pint/600 ml thick yogurt
4 oz/125 g cream cheese
3 tablespoons cointreau
2 tablespoons thin honey

Dissolve the sugar in the coffee, combine all the ingredients and freeze in a covered container.

COFFEE AND NUT TORTA

4 oz/125 g butter
6 oz/175 g sugar
2 eggs, beaten
1 teaspoon baking powder
6 oz/175 g plain flour
3 fl oz/75 ml espresso coffee
8 oz/250 g walnuts, chopped

Cream the butter and sugar until light, then beat in the eggs. Add the baking powder to the flour and sieve into the butter mixture, alternating with the coffee. Beat until smooth and add the nuts. Butter an 8 in/20 cm cake tin and line the bottom with buttered baking parchment. Pour in the batter and bake in a preheated oven, 180°C/350°F/gas 4, for 45 minutes.

BAKED RICOTTA PUDDING

12 oz/375 g ricotta
3 eggs, separated
4 oz/125 g caster sugar
1 teaspoon cinnamon
3 fl oz/75 ml strong coffee
2 oz/50 g walnuts, chopped

Blend the ricotta, egg yolks, 3 oz/75 g sugar and the cinnamon in a food processor or whisk together in a bowl. Stir in the coffee and the walnut pieces. Whisk the egg whites until they stand in peaks and add the remaining sugar. Fold into the ricotta mixture and pour into a 2 pint/1 litre buttered mould, which should not be more than half full to allow for the pudding to rise. Bake in a preheated oven, 180°C/350°F/gas 4, for about 50 minutes, until the pudding is firm. Turn off the oven and leave the pudding in it until ready to serve; it is less likely to collapse.

COFFEE CHEESECAKE

6 oz/175 g butter
6 oz/175 g digestive biscuits, crushed
5 oz/150 g sugar
12 oz/375 g curd cheese
12 oz/375 g cream cheese
3 eggs
3 tablespoons very finely ground coffee
2 tablespoons plain flour
3 tablespoons cornflour
$^1/_2$ teaspoon salt
1 teaspoon cinnamon
$^3/_4$ pint/450 ml sour cream

to 190°C/375°F/gas 5 for a further 40 minutes. Check that the top is not browning too much, and if necessary cover with greased paper. Turn off the oven and leave the cheesecake in it for 1 hour. Refrigerate when cool.

Melt the butter and use a little to grease an 8 or 9 in/20–23 cm springform tin.
Stir half the butter into the biscuits with 3 oz/75 g sugar and spread the mixture in the tin to make a base.
Mix together the curd and cream cheese. Beat the eggs with the remaining sugar until pale, then add to the cheeses. Mix all the dry ingredients and stir them into the mixture. Now add the remaining butter and the sour cream.
Pour the mixture into the tin and bake in a preheated oven, 160°C/325°F/gas 3 for 15 minutes, then increase the heat

SOUR CREAM COFFEE CAKE

4 oz/125 g pecan nuts
1½ teaspoons cinnamon
2 oz/50 g soft brown sugar
5 oz/150 g granulated sugar
5 oz/150 g butter
4 egg yolks
¼ pint/150 ml sour cream
3 tablespoons very finely ground coffee
7 oz/200 g plain flour
1 teaspoon baking powder
½ teaspoon baking soda

Chop the nuts coarsely and combine with the cinnamon, brown sugar and 1 oz/25 g granulated sugar, or whizz them all together for a few seconds in a food processor.
Cream the rest of the sugar and the butter until light and fluffy. Beat in the egg yolks and then the sour cream. Sift together the coffee, flour, baking powder and baking soda and beat into the cream mixture, a little at a time. Butter an 8 in/20 cm springform tin and line the bottom with buttered baking parchment. Pour in half of the batter, top with most of the nut filling, then spread the rest of the batter over it. Sprinkle with the rest of the nut mixture and bake in a preheated oven, 180°C/350°F/gas 4, for about 1 hour. Cover with buttered paper for the last 15 minutes if the cake is browning too quickly.

ELINOR'S FUDGE CAKE

2 oz/50 g butter
2 oz/50 g caster sugar
1 egg, beaten
2 oz/50 g plain flour
$1/4$ teaspoon baking powder
$2^1/2$ tablespoons instant coffee
3 oz/75 g icing sugar
1 tablespoon water
1 oz/25 g butter
1 oz/25 g granulated sugar

Cream the butter and caster sugar and beat in the egg. Sift together the flour, baking powder and $1^1/2$ tablespoons coffee and fold into the egg mixture. Butter a 6 in/15 cm sandwich tin and bake in a preheated oven, 180°C/350°F/gas 4, for 20–25 minutes. To make the icing, sift the icing sugar into a bowl. Put the remaining coffee, the water, butter and granulated sugar in a small pan and bring to the boil. Pour onto the icing sugar and mix thoroughly. When cold beat until fluffy and spread over the top of the cake.

COFFEE CHOCOLATE CHIP COOKIES

4 oz/125 g butter
2 oz/50 g soft brown sugar
3 tablespoons instant coffee
2 tablespoons warm water
1 egg, beaten
5 oz/150 g plain flour
2 oz/50 g ground almonds
5 oz/150 g plain chocolate, chopped finely

Beat the butter and sugar together until light and creamy. Dissolve the coffee in the water and stir into the butter and sugar. Add the egg and beat well. Sift in the flour, then add the almonds and chocolate. Butter two baking trays and put spoonfuls of the mixture onto them, spaced well apart. Spread them a little with the back of the spoon. Bake in a preheated oven, 180°C/350°F/gas 4, for 15 minutes.

COFFEE TRUFFLES

3 oz/75 g butter
2 egg yolks
2 tablespoons icing sugar
8 oz/250 g plain chocolate
2 tablespoons very finely ground coffee
cocoa

Beat together the butter, egg yolks and icing sugar until creamy. Melt the chocolate over a pan of hot water. Add the chocolate and coffee to the butter mixture, beating and kneading until the mixture has thickened.
Form into small balls and dip them in cocoa powder.

INDEX

ACKNOWLEDGEMENTS

*The publishers
would like to thank
the following:*

· TYPESETTING ·
TRADESPOOLS LTD
FROME

PHOTOGRAPHIC
· ASSISTANCE ·
JONATHAN BUCKLEY

JACKET
· PHOTOGRAPHY ·
DAVE KING

· ILLUSTRATOR ·
JANE THOMSON

· REPRODUCTION ·
COLOURSCAN
SINGAPORE

PAGE 7 CHRISTIE'S LONDON, THE BRIDGEMAN ART LIBRARY
PAGE 9 (TOP) PETER NEWARK'S HISTORICAL PICTURES
(BOTTOM) MUSEO CIVICO CORRER, VENICE, THE BRIDGEMAN ART LIBRARY
PAGE 10 BRITISH MUSEUM, LONDON, THE BRIDGEMAN ART LIBRARY
PAGES 11, 18, 20 MARY EVANS PICTURE LIBRARY, LONDON
PAGES 12, 25 MARTIN BREESE, RETROGRAPH ARCHIVE, LONDON

CYNTHIA HOLE FOR PICTURE RESEARCH
ELINOR BREMAN AND JUNE KING FOR PREPARING FOOD
TAYLORS OF HARROGATE, TEA BLENDERS & COFFEE MERCHANTS
THE ALGERIAN COFFEE STORES, LONDON
E. SWONNELL, LONDON (SILVER COFFEE POT)
JON BLAKE, MAP ARTWORK, PAGES 12–13

ROSIE FORD FOR ADDITIONAL HELP

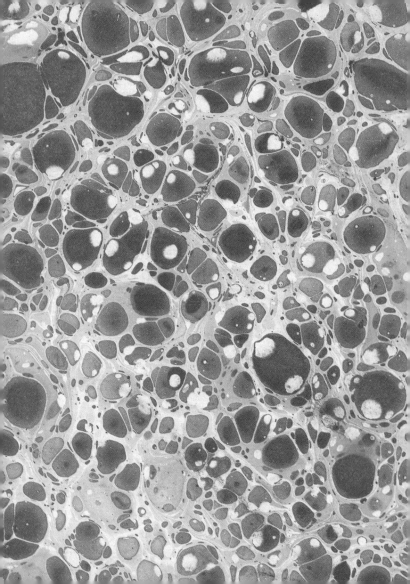